Christmas Program Builder

No. 53

LILLENAS DRAMA

Christmas Program Builder

No. 53

Creative Resources for Program Directors

Compiled by Kimberly R. Messer

Lillenas PUBLISHING COMPANY

KANSAS CITY, MO 64141

Contents

RECITATIONS

Preschool

Christmas Dawn

No wonder all seems rare and
    bright.
Jesus came to earth that night.
        —*Janet Lombard*

Happy Bells

Happy Bells are ringing,
    Listen to the sound,
Spreading Christmas cheer
    Here and all around.
        —*Robert Colbert*

Tell It

Run to and fro,
    Tell it wherever you go;
Christ the Lord is born!
    The whole world should know.
        —*Robert Colbert*

Happy Day

Happy birthday, Jesus.
    Thank You for blessing us so.
I want to share Your love
    Everywhere I go.
        —*Mary Ann Green*

Ain't That Good News!

Hooray! Hooray!
    Christ is born.
Ain't that good news
    This Christmas morn!
        —*Robert Colbert*

Christ-time Blessings

God has given
    To us His Son,
Christ-time blessings
    To everyone.
        —*Robert Colbert*

The Headlines

The headlines read
    A King is born.
Come worship Christ
    This Christmas morn!
        —*Robert Colbert*

Jesus, Jesus, Little One

*(Sung to the tune of
"Twinkle, Twinkle, Little Star")*
Jesus, Jesus, little one;
You are my God's only Son.
You were sent from heaven high,
Down to earth so You may die.
Jesus, Jesus, little one;
Thank You, God, for Your dear Son.
        —*Amy Spence*

A Manger Instead

Not in a mansion
    Or a King's bed,
Christ was born
    In a stable instead.
        —*Robert Colbert*

Gift from God

CHILD 1: In Bethlehem
Far away,
A Savior is born
This Christmas day.
CHILD 2: He lies in a manger
Upon the hay.
'Tis a Gift from God.
Hooray! Hooray!
—*Robert Colbert*

Grace and Truth

Christ our King
Of glory has come.
Grace and truth
To everyone.
—*Robert Colbert*

Welcome

We welcome you
This Christmas Season.
Jesus is born.
That's the reason.
—*Mary Ann Green*

Christmas Joy

Christ is born,
Mary's baby Boy,
God's living word,
Earth's Christmas joy!
—*Robert Colbert*

God Bless Us Everyone

FIRST CHILD: Where?
SECOND CHILD: In Bethlehem.
FIRST CHILD: Who?
SECOND CHILD: Christ is born.
FIRST CHILD: When?
SECOND CHILD: This Christmas morn.
BOTH: God bless us everyone.
FIRST CHILD: Say it again.
BOTH: God bless us everyone.
—*Robert Colbert*

A Special Way

God sent His love
In a special way
By giving His Son
On Christmas day!
—*Robert Colbert*

A Blessing

This Christmas Eve,
may peace descend
like stardust on your soul.
—*Janet Lombard*

Christmas

CHILD 1: Christmas comes in December,
That's how we remember.
CHILD 2: Jesus came years ago
Because He loved us so.
—*Mary Ann Green*

8

I'm Not Big

I'm not very big. But I have a big
   wish for you.
Happy Birthday, Jesus, and Merry
   Christmas, too.
          —Mary Ann Green

The Greatest Joy

The greatest joy
   On Christmas morn,
Is telling the world
   That Christ is born.
          —Robert Colbert

Heaven Above

Jesus came down
   From heaven above
To bless us with
   The Father's love.
          —Robert Colbert

We Wish

We wish you cheer
And happiness all through the year.
          —Mary Ann Green

Teensy Weensy

I'm a teensy weensy
   Bitsy shy,
So Merry Christmas,
   And to all, good-bye.
(Child waves and exits.)
          —Robert Colbert

Jesus Was His Name

(Sung to the tune of "B-I-N-G-O")
There was a baby born for us,
And Jesus was His name, yes!

(Chorus)
J-E-S-U-S
J-E-S-U-S
J-E-S-U-S
And Jesus was His name, yes!

This Baby grew to be a king,
The Savior of the world.

(Chorus)
This king, He died; He died for us.
He died upon a tree.

(Chorus)
This Savior, He will come again,
Return for all His children.

(Chorus)
          —Amy Spence

Ages 6 to 8

My Wish for You

Sometimes I feel big; *(spreads hands)*
Sometimes I feel small. *(Holds
thumb and second finger close to-
gether)*
Sometimes I feel short; *(holds hand
close to waist)*
Sometimes I feel tall. *(Holds hand
above head)*
But what does it matter, for all I can
say,
"I wish you a happy Christmas Day."
—*Margaret Primrose*

The Word of God

The word of God is Christ,
Who came from heaven above
To share with all the earth
God's everlasting love.
—*Robert Colbert*

Christmas Wish

I made a little wish
Upon a Christmas star
I saw shining in the sky
Above the heavens far.

It seemed to be much brighter
Than the others hanging 'round.
So I stood upon my tiptoes
And whispered from the ground,

"Star of Christmas,
Star of Light,
Fill the earth
With peace tonight!"
—*Enelle Eder*

Thank You, Lord

Thank You for the shepherds
Who hurried to the stall
Where they found the Child
Who came to save us all.

Thank You for the star
That shone in the sky at night.
And thank You for the wise men
Who followed its bright light.

Thank You, Lord, that Christmas
Is a very special season.
Our special love for You
Will always be the reason.
—*Margaret Primrose*

Christmas

C—C is for the Christ child.
H—H is for herald angels that sang.
R—R is for remembering Him.
I—I is for Israel's newborn King.
S—S is for the smiles we share.
T—T is for the tiny Babe in the
manger laid.
M—M is for the miracle when Jesus
came to earth.
A—A is for the animals that
watched Him that day.
S—S is for the Savior born that
Christmas day.
—*Mary Ann Green*

The Wise Men's Prayers

FIRST: For riches far greater than I
could hold,
I thank You, Jesus, and
bring You gold.
What a wonder it is to be
led by a star
And the One who always
knows where we are!

SECOND: Incense has been my great-
est treasure,
But now I have wealth too
great to measure,
Here are the spices I cast at
Your feet
For only You make my life
complete.

THIRD: Myrrh I bring as a gift to
You
Who came as King, but as
Savior too.
Before You now, I confess
my need
For You are the King of
Kings indeed.
—*Margaret Primrose*

A Christmas Prayer

Jesus, through my pain and strife,
bring Your light into my life.
Let Your Christmas glow pervade.
Make me calm and unafraid.
Through my trouble and despair,
let me sense Your mercy there.
May Your nativity delight,
a precious candle in the night.
—*Janet Lombard*

The Miracle of the Christmas Stocking

CHILD 1: This story was told ages
and ages ago
When the landscape was
gleaming with lots of
snow.

CHILD 2: Children hung their stockings on a starry night,
Hoping that morning
would bring their
hearts' delight!

CHILD 3: One little child was dili-
gently taught
That an eternal gift could
not be bought.

CHILD 4: Kneeling by the bed in the
calmness of night,
In the spirit of prayer,
there beamed a great
light!

CHILD 1: This one learned through
the years,
The Bible stories so loving
and dear—

CHILD 2: And found that the stock-
ing was filled with
care,
Giving heartfelt gifts of
love to share!

CHILD 3: An innocent heart over-
flowed with wonder-
ful news,
After Joseph and Mary en-
tered Bethlehem to
pay dues—

CHILD 4: Learning of the Christ
child's miracle birth,
How *Love* was sent down
from heaven to earth!

CHILD 1: Now that the holy Christmas season is here,

ALL: And our hearts are warmed and filled with cheer,
CHILD 2: May *all* stockings be hung with loving care,
ALL: And may each contain the *miracle story to share!*
—*Lorene Beeler*

Like Mary and Joseph

I hate the ride to Grandma's;
  It seems to take all day.
When I get tired of riding,
  I want to stop and play.

But what if we had no car,
  And I had to walk for a week?
Or ride a stubborn donkey
  Who threw me in the creek?

And what if we had to sleep
  On a pile of hay in a stall?
Well, we'd be like Mary and
    Joseph—
  That wouldn't be bad after all.
—*Margaret Primrose*

Christmas Shopping

Let me put patience on my list,
  and extra love for all—
gifts that will last, straight from my
  heart,
  and not straight from the mall.
—*Janet Lombard*

We Bring Our Hearts

FIRST CHILD: Hearts stand for love,
So here's one I bring
To say that I love
The newborn King.
SECOND CHILD: I, too, brought a heart
To hang on the tree,
For I love Jesus,
And He loves me.
THIRD CHILD: Now here's my heart.
I just want to say
That I love the Baby
Who slept on the hay.
FOURTH CHILD: We all love Jesus,
And all will take part
As we sing to Him
And hang these hearts.
ALL: *Be near me, Lord Jesus; I ask Thee to stay*
Close by me forever, and love me, I pray.
Bless all the dear children in Thy tender care,
And fit us for heaven, to live with Thee there.
*Stanza three, "Away in a Manger"
—*Margaret Primrose*

12

An Angel Announced

An angel announced
  The Savior's birth;
Good news came down
  From heaven to earth.

'Tis Christ the Lord,
  Our hope, and love,
The Father's gift
  And promise from above.
            —*Robert Colbert*

Something Better

I didn't see the angels
  When night became like day.
I didn't follow the shepherds
  To Jesus' bed of hay.
I didn't meet the wise men
  Who came from a land far away.
I didn't talk to Mary
  Nor listen to her pray.
But there's something far more im-
  portant
  Than hearing the angels sing.
It's giving my life to Jesus
  And serving Him as King.
            —*Margaret Primrose*

Christmas Sights

Cookies in the oven,
  Presents under the tree,
Candles in the windows,
  Children laughing with glee.

Fragrant wreaths are hanging;
  Carols fill the air.
Twinkling lights are shining;
  Christmas is everywhere!

The smells, sights, and symbols
  Are all wondrous to behold.
The wise men from the East
  Bring their gifts of gold.

But before the season passes,
  Take a quiet moment to
Remember the real purpose—
  God sent His Son to you!
            —*Enelle Eder*

What Matters Most

"Jesus was born in a basket,"
  I heard a little girl say,
And I didn't want to laugh
  About Jesus' bed of hay.

But then as she looked at a card
  With a manger in a stall,
She said what really matters:
  "Jesus loves us all."
            —*Margaret Primrose*

Ages 9 to 11

The Wise Man's Story

I'm one of the wise men,
  So wealthy and wise.
We followed a star
  That was placed in the skies.
We traveled a long way
  And stopped to see Herod the
  King.
We asked, "Where is Jesus,
  Have you heard or seen?"
Herod sent us to Bethlehem
  To look for the Child.
He seemed very upset,
  Perhaps even riled.
He told us to return
  When our mission was complete.
He said he wanted to
  Worship at Jesus' feet.
And so we traveled on,
  Following the bright star.
Soon our journey ended,
  It wasn't very far.
We found the young Child,
  We knew where we were,
And we gave Him our gifts
  Of gold, frankincense, and myrrh.
God warned in a dream,
  "Don't go to Herod again,"
For he was quite evil
  And so full of sin.
So then we departed
  And headed for home.
We chose another route
  For our camels to roam.
We knew Jesus would be safe
  From Herod's cruel sting,
For God would take care of
  The world's only King!
—*Wanda E. Brunstetter*

King of All Kings

He was not born in a castle
  With riches at His feet.
But came to a lowly manger
  Surrounded by hay so sweet.
He wasn't clothed in purple,
  Like most other royalty.
Nor was He attended by servants
  To come at His beck and plea.

And on His precious fingers
  There were no regal rings.
But that Baby truly was
  The King of all the Kings!
—*Enelle Eder*

I Will Lift My Eyes

Why didn't King Herod see the star
  That led toward the West from the
  East?
Why didn't he know that Jesus will
  save
  The greatest or the least?

Could it be that all he ever saw
  Were the things that gold could
  buy?
Did he care so much for the things
  of earth
  That he never would lift an eye?

Though I can't see with my two lit-
  tle eyes
  All the glories of heaven above,
I believe in the God who made the
  stars
  And thank Him for His love.

Optional: Read Psalm 121:1-2
—*Margaret Primrose*

The Christmas Tree

Christmas trees stand stately
  With branches lifted bold,
Adorned with shiny tinsel
  And balls of red and gold.

Twinkling lights surround them
  With garland in between,
But a message can be taken
  From those boughs of evergreen.

The beauty of their foliage
  Does not fade away.
Just like the Savior's love
  That keeps us day by day.

He is ever-faithful.
  Ever-loving, ever-true.
He came to save all people,
  And He cares about you!
      —Enelle Eder

The Shepherd's Story

I'm one of the shepherds
  Who cares for the sheep.
One night in the fields
  I fell fast asleep.
When suddenly, I was awakened
  By the sound of a voice.
It was an angel
  With news to rejoice.
He told of a baby
  Born in a town nearby.
Then other angels came, too,
  And I wondered why.

They told all us shepherds
  To go find the new King.
Then all of the angels
  Began to praise God and sing.
We left all our flocks
  And went with great haste
To a stable in Bethlehem
  Where the Baby was placed.
We bowed down to worship
  The Child we went to meet.
He was God's only Son,
  So perfect and sweet.
      —Wanda E. Brunstetter

Tag's Christmas

I'm glad I'm not a kitten,
  But I think that Tag has fun,
Chasing a roll of ribbon
  And trying to make it run.

She peeks around the presents
  While I rattle the ones on the
    floor.
Her ears point up when she hears
  The bells we put on the door.

She doesn't know a thing
  About the Savior's birth
Nor understand the reason
  That Jesus came to earth.

I like her anyway,
  So I just let her purr
While I read the Christmas story
  And pat her fur.
      —Margaret Primrose

No Room

There was no room in Bethlehem
 That night so long ago.
The town was filled with travelers,
 The sky with stars aglow.

Young Mary was so tired,
 Her journey had been long.
So they settled for a stable
 Away from the noisy throng.

And there her precious Baby
 Was born that holy night.
Into this world of darkness
 He came to bring us light.
 —*Enelle Eder*

The Angel's Story

I am one of the angels
 Who God sent to foretell.
I told lowly shepherds
 Where the new Baby would
  dwell.
I proclaimed to them all
 That Christ was the Lord.
I wanted them to know
 He should be loved and adored.
I said, "As a sign,
 You'll find Him in swaddling
  clothes.
He'll be lying in a manger,
 Where cattle low and the rooster
  crows."
Then with me were others
 From the heavenly host.
We gave glory to God,
 Praising Father, Son, and Holy
  Ghost.
We sang glory in the highest,
 And on earth, peace to all.
Goodwill toward all men,
 Both great and small!
 —*Wanda E. Brunstetter*

SKETCHES, PLAYS, & PROGRAMS

Come to the Manger
Robert Allen

Cast:
12 preschool children
Offstage VOICE

Scene:
A manger sits alone at the front of the sanctuary. The children will enter down the aisle and gather around the manger.

(Each CHILD enters, carrying a sign, and walks down to the front, kneeling near the manger. The lines for each CHILD are meant to be written on the sign and not to be spoken.)

FIRST CHILD: Come and see!

SECOND CHILD: Follow us!

THIRD CHILD: It's a baby!

FOURTH CHILD: He's here!

FIFTH CHILD: Peace on Earth!

SIXTH CHILD: A child is born!

SEVENTH CHILD: Come with us!

EIGHTH CHILD: Don't miss Him!

NINTH CHILD: His name is Jesus!

TENTH CHILD: He's the Savior!

ELEVENTH CHILD: Let's go!

TWELFTH CHILD: Come to the manger!

(When all the CHILDREN have gathered around the manger, the offstage VOICE speaks.)

VOICE: "Out of the mouth of babes and sucklings hast thou ordained strength . . . and a little child shall lead them."

The end

The Little Drummer Boy

(A one-act children's skit)

Amy Spence

Cast:
> LITTLE DRUMMER BOY (LDB)
> 4 COWS
> 4 DONKEYS
> 2 KITTENS
> 4 HORSES

Costumes:

The Little Drummer Boy (LDB) should have costuming similar to that of a shepherd. He should also carry a simple drum strapped across his shoulder and be holding a pair of rustic drumsticks. For the animals, children can wear touches of costume to help represent each animal. You can make this elaborate or as simple as your resources allow. Face paint or masks work great.

Production notes:

This simple one-act play is designed to be performed with minimal costuming and props. It can also be staged by younger or even older students, both completely capable of accomplishing a great performance.

(Before the skit begins, you may want to have the cast come up onstage to the piano softly playing "The Little Drummer Boy." This makes a nice introduction.)

LDB: Hello there! The folks here in Bethlehem call me the Little Drummer Boy. My animals and I are off to see the newborn King, Baby Jesus. We are going to bring Him the finest gifts we can find. *(He pauses and thinks for a moment.)* Wait a minute! I don't think we have any gifts to give Him. Cows, do you have any gifts to give Baby Jesus?

COW NO. 1: All I have is this rusted old cowbell. Will that do?

LDB: No; do you have anything better?

COW NO. 2: How about some of that hay over there in our manger? It's still fresh.

COW NO. 3: No! *(Almost yelling)* We need something more than hay. We can give Him a bucket of water too.

COW NO. 4: Mooooo . . .ve over! Our Little Drummer Boy needs something special. Let's ask the donkeys. Maybe they have something that would honor Jesus. *(Looks over at the DONKEYS)* Donkeys, do you have anything?

DONKEY NO. 1: Hee-haw! Did you say you needed something special? I've got a lovely warm blanket in the stable.

DONKEY NO. 2: That old thing is not lovely and hardly warm! *(Looking at DONKEY NO. 3)* What about you?

DONKEY NO. 3: No, I don't think so. I've only got this worn-out old bridle. Jesus deserves more than that.

DONKEY NO. 4: OH! Most definitely! How about if we give Him a ride into Bethlehem?

LDB: That would be nice—but soon enough. Kittens, do you have anything to give our newborn King?

KITTEN NO. 1: Nothing much. Just this old ball of yarn. It's a beautiful color, maybe we could make a nice blanket out of it.

KITTEN NO. 2: Oh yes, that would be perrrr . . . fect! What do you think, Little Drummer Boy?

LDB: That would be nice, too, but I was thinking of something a little more special.

HORSE NO. 1 *(butting in on the conversation):* Special . . . did you say? I'm pretty special! I'm the fastest horse this side of Judaea.

HORSE NO. 2: You are not! I can outrun you to the stable any day.

HORSE NO. 3: OK . . . OK . . . you two. *(Trying to get them calmed down)* We need to help our boy find something special for Baby Jesus.

HORSE NO. 4: I think I have an idea! Since none of us have anything that's really worth something, I think we should give Jesus the one thing we have that is priceless.

LDB: Yes! You're right! We must give Jesus our hearts. Come, let us go and worship the newborn King. (LDB *waves all of the animals offstage to give Baby Jesus their hearts.)*

And the Animals Sing

Eileen M. Berger

Cast:
- NARRATOR
- HEN
- CHICKS
- HORSE
- LAMB
- DUCK
- COW
- CAMEL
- DOVE
- DONKEY
- 3 SHEPHERDS

NARRATOR: It was evening and the animals in the village of Bethlehem were getting ready for sleep. There was the mother hen . . .

HEN: Cluck, cluck! Come into the stable, my little ones. Gather close and close your eyes.

CHICKS: Peep, peep!

NARRATOR: The big, strong horse stopped eating grass and came in . . .

HORSE: Neigh, neigh! I carried a big fat man on my back for many miles and I am tired. Neigh!

NARRATOR: And a soft, cuddly lamb . . .

LAMB: It's time for me to stay safely in the stable. Baaa, baaa.

NARRATOR: And a noisy duck . . .

DUCK: Quack, quack! Quack, quack!

NARRATOR: And the pleasant cow . . .

COW: Moo, moo. I'm tired too.

NARRATOR: And a grumpy camel . . .

CAMEL: Grunt, grunt! Make room for me. *I* carried a wealthy businessman from far-off Egypt. Get out of my way! Grunt, grunt!

NARRATOR: And the gentle dove . . .

DOVE: Coo, coo! I will stay out of everyone's way in my nest up at the top of the wall.

NARRATOR: And a small gray donkey entered with a woman and a man beside him.

DONKEY: Hee-haw. I guess I am the last animal to get here, but see? The woman I carried on my back does not feel good. Will you please help fix a comfortable bed for her?

NARRATOR: All the animals set to work. The horse *("neigh, neigh")*, the camel *("grunt, grunt")*, the lamb *("baaa, baaa")*, and the cow *("mooo, mooo")* gathered sweet-smelling hay and spread it out. The duck *("quack, quack")* and the chicken *("cluck, cluck")* and the dove *("coo, coo")* fluttered around, making the soft bed nice and smooth.

The donkey *("hee-haw")* walked with the woman, whose name was Mary, over to the bed of hay, and her husband, Joseph, helped her to lie down. The animals all said "Goodnight, sleep well," as animals do *(All animal sounds)*, and they went to sleep themselves.

But after a while all of them woke up, for they heard something they'd never heard here before. It was the sound of a baby crying! Something wonderful had happened! Mary and Joseph were very happy to have the newly born baby Boy with them, and they gave Him the name *Jesus*. Mary held Him in her arms and hummed a little song, and the animals all tried to sing too. *(All animal sounds)*

Some shepherds came into the stable, all excited.

SHEPHERD NO. 1: Angels came to us, out on the hillside . . .

SHEPHERD NO. 2: They told us about a baby born here tonight. He's to be wrapped in cloths and lying in a manger . . .

SHEPHERD NO. 3: This Baby is special. He will grow up to be our Savior, Christ the Lord . . .

NARRATOR: The shepherds got down on their knees to worship Jesus, and the horse, and the sheep, and the cow, and the donkey, and the camel got down on *their* knees too. The chicken and the duck and the dove fluttered around also. And they all sang this little song:

EVERYONE: Here in a manger, here in a stall,
You came to Bethlehem, came to us all.
We love you, Jesus, we're glad You came.
We're glad God sent You; we praise Your name.

The end

The Donkey's Story
Jean M. Soule

"Ee-yore, ee-yore!" A small brown donkey stood in one corner of the stable, braying loudly. He was watching his master talking to a man who had come into the barn that morning.

"What are they saying?" the donkey wondered. "Oh, the man is pointing at me and my master is shaking his head. Now they are coming over to my stall. What is happening?"

"This donkey is all I have left for hire," said the master, shaking his head. "He is not young, but he is still a good worker. You say you need him to go from here to Bethlehem? That is a long journey."

"He looks healthy," said the man. "I will take him. My wife and I must go to Bethlehem to pay our taxes. I will come tomorrow. Please have him ready for the trip."

The donkey brayed again. "I am to take a long journey? Why, I haven't been out on the road for quite a while. I hope the man will feed me well and take care of my hooves if I stumble."

The next morning the man came to the stable again. This time a young woman was with him, and they had some heavy bundles.

"Ee-yore!" said the donkey. "I will have to carry a hefty load."

Soon they were on the way. The woman was not too heavy, and she smiled at him and patted his head gently. He liked her, and the man was nice to him too.

They traveled for many miles, stopping at night in a cave or a shepherd's hut and sometimes at an inn. Finally, the donkey saw the houses and buildings of the town just over the hill.

"We are here at last, Mary," said Joseph (that was the man's name). "Soon we will have a comfortable room at the inn."

The lady smiled, but she looked very tired. The donkey hoped that tonight she would sleep well.

When the man inquired at the inn, he was told there was no room. People had come for miles around to pay their taxes to Rome.

"There is a stable behind my inn," said the innkeeper. "You are welcome to stay there for the night if you don't mind sleeping with the cattle and sheep."

Joseph told Mary there was no other place, so she agreed to stay there. They found the stable and a place where she could lie down to rest. Joseph prepared her a meal and something for the little donkey too. He saw to it that his beast had clean, dry straw for his bed.

The tired animal drowsed in the night, but as soon as it was morning, he heard a strange sound—a baby was crying in the manger nearby. Mary was lying there and Joseph was beside her looking at her with great love.

"Ee-yore!" the donkey said softly. "It must be a miracle. I knew I was carrying one person—but now there are two!"

Mary turned and looked at the donkey. She reached out her hand to him and said, "Since you brought Him here, you should be the first to see Him. He is a very special child, and I thank you for carefully bringing both of us to this stable."

"Ee-yore!" said the donkey as he nudged Mary's hand and looked at her beautiful face. "I am proud to have been the one to bring Him to His birthplace!"

The end

The Chief Priest

Margaret Primrose

I am one of the chief priests who served in the magnificent temple in the Holy City, Jerusalem. It's important to remember that God himself set apart the chief priests for His special service.

Try to imagine our shock when a caravan of heathen stargazers, also known as magi or magicians, arrived from the East and asked: "Where is He that is born King of the Jews?" God wouldn't tell them something He hadn't shown us about the Promised One. He wouldn't lead them to worship Him. We Jews are His chosen people. Of course, we dared not ask a question that would have enraged King Herod, but why did the magi go to him first? It just showed their ignorance.

King Herod was very upset, of course. No rival was going to stand in his way! Yet he would claim to worship God just as long as it seemed to be to his advantage.

We chief priests and scribes were all summoned to meet with King Herod and the foreigners—I do not call them wise men. Of course, we hurried to the palace. We did not want to lose our heads. And we told Herod what we could all agree upon from our search of the Scripture; the prophet Micah had named the place of birth of the long-promised One many, many years before then. It was to be in Bethlehem.

Why King Herod should have been so afraid of a baby was hard to believe. Herod would be an old, old man before any child had time to become a man.

For an insane moment I wanted to join the magi as King Herod sent them to Bethlehem to find the Babe. Maybe I was just curious about them and their long fanatical journey. Maybe I was bored, and it sounded like an adventure. But, no, it was not for a priest to link himself with a band like that. Nor did I think it wise to make the seven-mile trip by myself.

Since then I've heard a tale about ignorant sheepherders who were visited by angels about the time the magi saw the star. One of the angels is supposed to have said that a Savior had just been born in a stable in Bethlehem. It's pure nonsense, just an example of how one wild report can be the starter for another.

Well, we haven't heard any more about the so-called wise men who were supposed to find a baby and report to Herod. They fled the country, it seems. That made Herod furious. Now he's trying to kill every little boy two years old or under. None of them will grow up to replace him if he can help it. It's too bad, but what can we do?

Oh, I didn't tell you my name. It's . . . *(extends his hand)* But what does it matter? There's nobody here. Nobody who thinks it's important to know.

The end

The Wise Man

Margaret Primrose

It's still a mystery how God used a star to tell the other wise men and me that Jesus, the King of the Jews, had been born. We come from a country where most stargazers worship false gods. Yet we were convinced that we should worship the new King and that the star would lead us to Him.

Those who have never crossed the desert on a humpy, swaying camel can little imagine our long, hard journey—the nights of following the star, the fear of being mistaken as a band of robbers, the homesickness. And the hot winds that not only shifted the desert sand but threw it in our food, in our clothes, and in our faces. Then the star disappeared.

Yet, we kept on because we were determined. We were headed toward Jerusalem, the holy city of the Jews, and there we should find the King.

When at last we neared Jerusalem, our boredom turned to excitement. It built to a peak as our weary camels lumbered into the Holy City. We asked the first merchant we could find where we should go to see the King of the Jews.

The man's blank stare was a shock to us. He knew nothing of the King. Nor, it appeared, did anyone else in the whole city of Jerusalem. Yet by and by we were summoned into the presence of King Herod.

We did not know his reputation—that it was safer to be his pig than his son, and that he would try to kill the Child. He claimed to have become one who worships only God. It was puzzling that he, even he, knew nothing about the new King we came to worship.

Herod called together all the chief priests and scribes—all of them, mind you—and demanded to know where the Promised One would be born. There was a flurry of searching through their sacred writings, but in the end, they all agreed. Bethlehem it was. A prophet named Micah had foretold it many many years before then.

King Herod sent us to Bethlehem to find the Child. Not even one of the scribes or priests offered to join us, though it was a distance of only seven miles. But we took Herod at his word when he said he, too, wanted to worship the King when we found Him.

By then we imagined a door-to-door search and feared that both we and our treasures were at risk in a foreign land. There were probably too many people who knew the custom of lavishing gifts upon new rulers, and, of course, we brought the best our country had to offer. How would we know when we had found the real King? If we offered our gold, frankincense, and myrrh to the wrong Child, there would be no exchange of gifts. We would go home with much less than we came.

But an amazing thing happened. The star we had seen in the East suddenly reappeared. It not only led us directly to the right house but stood over the house. We felt ready to explode with joy.

It wasn't enough to kneel before Him. We worshiped with our faces in the dust of the dirt floor. It did not matter that the family was poor and could give us nothing in return for our gifts. We worshiped the King of Kings! Nothing will ever be the same since we found Him.

The end

Lord, in This New Year

Faye Nyce

LEADER: "O LORD, you have searched me
    And you know me.
You know when I sit and when I rise;
    You perceive my thoughts from afar.
You discern my going out and my lying down;
    You are familiar with all my ways.
Before a word is on my tongue
    You know it completely, O LORD" (Psalm 139:1-4).

GROUP 1: We have known that God was with us in the past.
We have experienced His grace and mercy.

GROUP 2: The old year is history—gone—never to be retrieved.
The hand of the Lord has been upon us.

LEADER: Have we been a faithful people to the Lord
In this year that is now past?
Have we called upon Him in our time of need?

GROUP 1: We have known both joy and blessing
As we have endeavored to walk in His ways.
The mighty arm of the Lord has reached out to us.

GROUP 2: But there have also been hurts that must be healed.
Like a time bomb ticking away, they fester;
Ready to explode in our midst, without notice.

LEADER: Lord, we entreat you today,
At the outset of a New Year—at a time of new beginnings.
You know our thoughts and words before we communicate any-
    thing.

GROUP 1: Deliver us, Lord, from our pain with one another.
Give us grace to possess the humility
We need to confess to one another.

GROUP 2: We desire forbearance with each other,
That we not judge one another harshly.

LEADER: To the wise God, our caring Father, we ask:

GROUP 1: For your blessing upon our lives,
That we be slow to speak, quick to listen, swift to care.

GROUP 2: Choosing to live lives after the very heart of God,
Knowing He will guide us in His way.

ALL: As we enter this new year, we declare as Joshua of old once said, "As for me and my household, we will serve the Lord."

The end

Away in a Manger
Jeff Hinman

Theme: Christmas. Cute baby or awesome God? The hope that Christ brought.

Scripture: Isaiah 9:2, 6-7; Luke 1:30-35

Cast:
> PLAYER 1—Believing Shepherd
> PLAYER 2—Skeptical Shepherd

Setting:
> New Testament. Birth of Jesus.

(PLAYER 1 *and* PLAYER 2 *enter. Both are shepherds. Need sticks or something to show this.* PLAYER 1 *points to the "manger" as if it is directly in front of them. An actual manger may be used if there is budget. Otherwise, let the imagination set the scene.*)

PLAYER 1 *(excited and happy, pointing to the manger):* See, there He is, just like I told you!

PLAYER 2 *(less enthusiastic and skeptical):* Well, it's a baby in a manger all right. *(Pauses and looks more closely)* He is kind of cute . . . *(breaks into baby talk)* How are you little baby-waby? Oh, is the little smoogy-woogy tired? You're a cute little bunny-wubby, aren't you?

PLAYER 1 *(smiling and confident):* He is the One who placed the stars in the heavens and set the planets in motion.

PLAYER 2: What? Who are you talking about?

PLAYER 1 *(surprised* PLAYER 2 *doesn't realize who the Baby is):* The Baby! He's the King of Kings and Lord of Lords!

PLAYER 2 *(not impressed):* How many kings and lords do you know who are born in a stable and set into a feeding trough? The King of Kings here better hope that the ol' cow of cows over there doesn't get hungry and take a bite out of Him!

PLAYER 1: But we saw the angels! They told us to come here! You can ask the others if you want!

PLAYER 2 *(looks at* PLAYER 1*'s forehead, concerned):* Have you been head-butting the rams again?

PLAYER 1 *(getting angry):* Knock it off!

PLAYER 2 *(trying to be reasonable):* Look, why would the King of Kings—the *Messiah*—allow himself to be born in a manger? I'm a shepherd and yet even I had a better place of birth than this!

PLAYER 1: I don't know. Maybe it lets us know that He didn't just come for the kings and rulers, but for us too, the poor and humble.

PLAYER 2 *(still being reasonable)*: Look, He's a cute kid and all . . .

PLAYER 1 *(interrupting with vigor)*: He's almighty God!

PLAYER 2 *(getting angry and vigorous too)*: He needs a diaper change!

PLAYER 1 *(trying to calm himself and PLAYER 2 down)*: Shh! You'll upset Him!

PLAYER 2 *(still sarcastic)*: Well we wouldn't want Him to start crying now, would we? The King of Kings here would make Noah's flood look like a puddle!

PLAYER 1 *(talking to the Baby)*: Ignore the bad man, Jesus. That's what I do.

PLAYER 2 *(calming down, looks at the Baby for a few moments)*: Well, there is something . . . special about Him. *(Looking at PLAYER 1)* To hear He's the Messiah from you, well . . . it's hard to believe. *(Looking back at the manger)* But to actually see Him . . . there is something . . . *(still fighting the idea)* But that this is God come in the flesh? As a Baby in a manger?

PLAYER 1: It's a paradox.

PLAYER 2 *(responding to PLAYER 1's understatement)*: Well, it certainly alters my worldview! *(Sighs)* I don't know, we'll see what He does with His life. It would be nice if He did turn out to be all you claim He is. I just hope things improve for Him. This manger is a pretty rough start.

PLAYER 1: I think it is a perfect start. The perfect start to a perfect life.

PLAYER 2: So you think He'll end up on Herod's throne, huh?

PLAYER 1: I don't know where He will end up. *(Looking close at the Baby)* But wherever it is—it will be the perfect place at the perfect time.

PLAYER 2 *(after a moment of silence, claps PLAYER 1 on the shoulder)*: We have sheep to tend.

PLAYER 1 *(straightens up, speaking to the Baby)*: When you get older, I'll show you how to tend sheep. (PLAYER 1 *and* PLAYER 2 *begin to exit.*)

PLAYER 2: Yeah, like the King of Kings will be a shepherd!

PLAYER 1: You never know. I think He'd make a good one!

(Exit)

The end

Christmas Memories
Robert Allen

Cast:
> NARRATOR—a young girl
> ELSIE—the narrator as a child
> BRUCE—her brother
> MR. GRANT—her father
> MRS. GRANT—her mother

Setting:
> The play takes place in the living room of the Grant home, which is decorated for Christmas.

(NARRATOR *stands to one side and observes the memories of her childhood as they occur.*)

NARRATOR: When I was a child, Christmas was the most exciting time of the year. Everything was exciting—the snow outside, the tree inside, the mysterious gifts in their colorful wrappings, the shopping trips to the mall, the Christmas program at church, relatives coming, the Christmas goodies Mother and I baked—everything was exciting. Even Bruce, my little brother, was exciting at Christmas. It didn't even bother me when he argued with me about how Christmas should be celebrated. It didn't bother me because *I* knew.

BRUCE: I think that this year we should open our presents on Christmas Eve.

ELSIE: No! No! No! We've always done it on Christmas morning. It's a family tradition.

BRUCE: But Dad's family didn't do it that way, did they, Dad?

MR. GRANT: That's right, Bruce. We always opened our gifts on Christmas Eve. Maybe we should do it that way this year.

ELSIE: No!

MRS. GRANT: Now Bruce, you and your father quit teasing Elsie. Of course we will wait until morning.

BRUCE: So we'll think it's Santa who is bringing the gifts?

MRS. GRANT: No, that's not the reason, though your grandfather always used to ring the bells we had on our tree while he filled our stockings just to make *us* think we had a Christmas visitor. I think we open them Christmas morning . . .

ELSIE: Because that's the way we've always done it.

NARRATOR: Every year Daddy and Bruce would try to talk us into opening just one present Christmas Eve. And then Daddy would start complaining about getting up early Christmas morning. This time Bruce was on my side.

MR. GRANT: Well, let's at least sleep in until 8:00 Christmas morning. There's no sense getting up early.

ELSIE: Daddy!

BRUCE: You know we won't be able to sleep that long.

MRS. GRANT: Give up, honey. You'll never convince them.

ELSIE: We have to get up early and put Christmas music on the record player and turn it up real loud.

BRUCE: And you have to pretend not to hear it so we can grab our stockings and come running in and jump on your bed to wake you up.

ELSIE: It's our family tradition.

NARRATOR: And then Daddy would just roll his eyes as if he was the most persecuted father in the world, but we knew he was grinning inside. Why, if we slept past 6:00, he would probably sneak out and turn on the record player himself. Christmas was so exciting that I didn't even get upset when Bruce couldn't remember whose turn it was to hand out the gifts.

BRUCE: I know Elsie did it last year.

ELSIE: No, I didn't. Marcie did it.

BRUCE: Marcie? Who's Marcie?

ELSIE: She's our cousin, silly.

MRS. GRANT: I think Elsie's right. My brother and his family were here last Christmas and I think we let Marcie hand out the gifts.

BRUCE: Then it's still my turn because that was Elsie's turn, and it has been two years since I did it.

MR. GRANT: It has been two years, Bruce, but since Elsie let Marcie do it last year, I think it would be her turn.

MRS. GRANT: Your father is right, Bruce. But I bet Elsie will give you the first gift.

NARRATOR: And of course, I did just that. It was hard sitting there and waiting for the rest of them to open their gifts, but that was the way we always did it. One person opened a gift while everyone else watched, and then it was the next person's turn. It took quite awhile, but it was a family tradition.

BRUCE: And now it's time for breakfast. I'm going to suck the juice from my orange through a candy cane.

32

ELSIE: You have to squeeze the orange first.

BRUCE: No, you don't! I tried it your way last year, and the skin just broke.

ELSIE: That's because you didn't squeeze it gently. You played catch with it —against the wall.

BRUCE: It takes too long your way.

ELSIE: But it works. If you don't squeeze the orange for a long time, it won't be juicy and then the candy cane won't work either.

NARRATOR: You might think that Bruce and I argued about everything, but really we didn't. And even when we did, it was kind of fun, almost like a family tradition. But there was one thing we never disagreed about.

MRS. GRANT: Before I serve breakfast, I think we should read the Christmas story.

MR. GRANT: An excellent idea. Who is going to read it this year?

BRUCE: Daddy!

ELSIE: Daddy!

MR. GRANT: All right! Here we go.

"And it came to pass in those days that a decree went out from Caesar Augustus that all the world should be registered. This census first took place while Quirinius was governing Syria.

"So all went to be registered, everyone to his own city. And Joseph also went up from Galilee, out of the city of Nazareth, into Judea, to the city of David, which is called Bethlehem, because he was of the house and lineage of David, to be registered with Mary, his betrothed wife, who was with child. So it was, that while they were there, the days were completed for her to be delivered.

"And she brought forth her firstborn Son, and wrapped Him in swaddling cloths, and laid Him in a manger, because there was no room for them in the inn." (Luke 2:1-7, NKJV)

NARRATOR: No one could read the Christmas story like Father. When he read about Bethlehem it seemed as if we were really there. And when he read about Jesus, it seemed like He was right there with us—and I guess He was.

The end

Looking In
Joan M. Burnside

Cast:

    JOE—30ish male, suit, expensive coat, enters talking into cell phone

    FRAN—60s female, gloves, hat, well coiffed, lugging Nordstrom's shopping bag

    DOROTHY—Fran's friend, 60s, well dressed, also with Nordstrom's shopping bag

    SIERRA—17ish, throw back from flower girl clothes, black boots, natural look, several earrings, hair in braids or corn rows

    MIKE—20s, jeans, tennies, polo shirt, pushing stroller with sleeping toddler, dragging Nieman's bags

    KAITLYN—Mike's wife, 20s, designer jeans, beautiful

    DANIELLE—sleeping 2-year-old in stroller (could use a large doll, covered with blankets)

    CHI—25, male, foreign grad student, backpack, should be done with a very pronounced accent

    DANIEL—5 years old, out shopping with Grandma

    NANCY—70s, Daniel's grandma

    VIC—Santa look-alike, has red and white Santa hat (original actor had a natural, very large, white beard) otherwise dressed normally

Setting:

Sidewalk in front of large department store with large window display. Scene in window is only described in scene by characters passing by. All enter from SR and work to CS, looking out as if viewing large window display.

Running time: 12 minutes

JOE (*walking hurriedly, with cell phone to ear*): Thanks, Ken. I'll get back to you on that. Just thought I'd get out of the office for a little break. (*Snaps cell phone closed and puts it away. Stops to gawk, starts talking out loud to whomever is near, stops as if looking at first window.*) Nice job on the color schemes. (*Moves on to next display*) Great job! (*Laughs*) Look at that! Palm Pilots hanging from the Christmas tree! (*Moves on to CS, stares, searching, then in disdain*) Well, . . . this one wins for the least exciting display on the block! You'd think in this day and age someone would have been able to be a little more innovative . . . nothing but a manger, some people, animals, and . . . a baby . . . and none of them move! This store's probably taken a nose dive this year, couldn't spring for a decent display. (*Pause*) How cheap can they get . . . hay and fake sheep. (*Pause*) Maybe there's a trick to it . . . like that angel's really a live model and he'll start singing anytime now. *(Beat)* Now *that* would be worth seeing. *(Pause)* Last year Macy's had some barking dogs, all dressed up like reindeer, it was the best. *(Pause)* Well, I can't wait forever, I guess no live action here . . . what a waste of space. *(Exits, stopping to look at displays to SL)*

FRAN *(enters with* DOROTHY *at her side, is very sophisticated and aloof):* How quaint, but why?

DOROTHY: Takes one back though, doesn't it? Do you remember when every town had a display like this out on the lawn in front of City Hall?

FRAN: I do, but now they're much more . . . ecumenical. We've progressed to include the overall spirit of the season—scenes of ice-skaters, snow-men, and family gatherings. Not so narrow-minded, you know?

DOROTHY *(hesitant):* Yes, progress and all . . . can't exclude people by being so specific. What is it all about anyway?

FRAN *(beginning to get huffy):* Whoever put this one out certainly wasn't in keeping with the times. I'm surprised they were allowed to get away with this. *(Pause)* Maybe we should write a note to the owners. I hoped people would have moved beyond this kind of mentality. Why must they bring in Jesus—excluding people during the holidays by focusing on one religion over another? If you ask me, it's pretty appalling!

DOROTHY: Oh Fran, don't let it get your dander up. *(Pause)* For some . . . this scene is inclusive . . . takes us all back to the humble beginnings of that first Christmas. Why let some sheep and a manger get your goat? *(Giggles then becomes reflective)* In a way, there are some things from the past I kind of miss. I for one don't get a chance to think about how it all began . . . I mean, how this season got its start. It's been a while since I thought about those stories my mom used to read me.

FRAN: Now, Dorothy, don't get maudlin on me. *(Pause)* That's just what I mean . . . we need more uplifting things to look at. *(Pause)* Come on . . . let's go on. I've heard Macy's has a wonderful scene of a home decorated for the holidays, all done in earth tones and recycled products. They're going to be giving away some aroma-therapy certificates at the spa downtown to a few lucky passersby.

DOROTHY: You go on . . . I'll catch up with you. *(Pause)* I'm not as spry as you are Fran. That's what I get for quitting that aerobics class . . . I'll be there in a moment. *(She hangs back to look as* FRAN *scurries away.)*

FRAN: Don't be long now, remember that new restaurant we wanted to try.

SIERRA *(staring at display, incredulous):* Whoa . . . now there's a new look. I've never seen one like that. *(Pause)* Who's the lady with the baby? What's with the hay?

35

DOROTHY *(quietly):* That's Mary, Jesus' mother.

SIERRA: Oh . . . yeah . . . *(hesitant)* I knew that . . . but how's that goin' to get them to sell anything? I mean, there's nothing here to make me want to go in and look around. *(Pause)* Like I'd want to buy that dress!

DOROTHY: Oh . . . I don't think that's their intent . . . I mean . . . to sell something with their display. *(Pause)* Somehow . . . I think they had more in mind.

SIERRA: Then what's the point? All the other ones have these incredible things in their windows that make you want to run right in and buy the stuff right off the mannequins!

DOROTHY: I'm not sure what the point is . . . why they're doing this. *(Pause)* I've been just standing here asking myself that same question.

SIERRA: Seems kind of lame to give up the space when they could use it to show off some of their clothes. But this . . . I don't get it . . . kind of back to nature with those sheep. *(Pause)* Maybe they have some new wool coats they're trying to push . . . you know . . . not offend the antifur people.

DOROTHY: Maybe. *(Pause)* Last year some women came and threw blood at some of the people from Nieman's because they still were selling furs. It was horrible.

SIERRA: Pretty radical. *(Pause)* You said it was Mary and Jesus . . . I've heard of them . . . I think.

DOROTHY: You know . . . Jesus, the Baby, the Christ child . . . that's where the word Christmas comes from.

SIERRA: Oh, thanks . . . I always wondered . . . just figured they were all part of the Santa thing. *(Pause)* Still think it's kind of weird . . . they could have done more with that star. I'd have used candles . . . everyone's into candles these days. Well, . . . have a good one. (SIERRA *exits, but* DOROTHY *remains, quietly reflecting.)*

KAITLYN *(reaches display excitedly):* Look, Mike . . . sheep . . . is Danielle awake? She loved the sheep at the petting zoo . . .

MIKE *(pushing stroller, dragging shopping bags and diaper bag):* No, she's finally asleep, and DON'T wake her up . . .

KAITLYN: But look how cute they look, even if they are fake . . .

MIKE *(irritated):* If she wakes up later, I can bring her back. *(Pause)* We spent two hours in the last store, and you said you just wanted to stop in for a second! Aren't you done with your list yet? I'm getting tired and hungry, and we only have one clean diaper left.

KAITLYN: Did you eat the granola bar I packed for you?

MIKE: Yes, *and* the goldfish crackers and Fruit Loops that probably weren't meant for me.

KAITLYN: Mike! Whatever happened to that patient guy I once dated? Before we were married you used to love to take me shopping.

MIKE: I was a fool for love back then. Now I'm tired and want to go home and put my feet up!

KAITLYN: You know, I think your job is making you a cranky old man way before your time.

MIKE: Well, maybe you'd like to go out and work for a living, and I'll stay home and play with the baby!

KAITLYN *(hurt, angry):* Is that what you think I do all day?

MIKE: Sometimes I wonder . . .

KAITLYN *(sarcastically):* Well, . . . I'm glad we had this little conversation. *(Beat)* It's nice to hear what you really think of me.

MIKE: Oh, lighten up . . .

KAITLYN: Seems like we got along a lot better when our lives were simpler . . . your job wasn't taking over your life! Look at those two. *(Motions toward window)* They didn't have much, but look at their faces. *(Pause)* We have it all and we're out here arguing in front of perfect strangers!

MIKE: So what? Do you want me to quit my job and raise sheep?

KAITLYN: You? . . . you don't even like my cat!

MIKE: What *do* you want, Kaitlyn?

KAITLYN: To stop arguing out here in front of everyone for one thing! *(Pause)* And maybe we need to look at our lives . . . I mean . . . I'm grateful that you make enough so that I can stay home with the baby, but if you're so stressed out . . . then maybe we need to see what we can do to simplify our lives. Maybe that's what the display case is telling us: "Hey folks out there, slow down . . . what's really important in life?"

MIKE: What is important in life?

KAITLYN: I'm not sure . . . but I know what we've got right now isn't really cutting it.

MIKE: So . . . you want to go home?

KAITLYN: I guess.

MIKE: I really need to eat something if we're going to have anymore of these conversations. I don't do well trying to reprioritize my life on an empty stomach. I'm afraid I'll cut out everything but the food budget!

KAITLYN: That's what you get for stopping in front of a display full of lamb chops. *(Pause)* But it was good . . . I mean that we came here.

MIKE *(from edge of SL, hurriedly)*: Are you coming?

KAITLYN *(sadly, longingly)*: Yes.

CHI *(as if reading sign overhead)*: "First Christmas." This is it . . . no tree, no presents? Where is the chimney for Santa to enter in? This is very odd . . . not what I thought at all. Nothing like commercials on TV show. No reindeer, just sheep . . . very different than what I've learned from friends. *(Turns to DOROTHY who has been standing silently nearby.)* Excuse me . . . could you explain this to me? Why no jolly Santa and little elves?

DOROTHY: Well, this is kind of an odd display . . . but actually . . . it is how Christmas began.

CHI: With family and baby?

DOROTHY: Yes, that's Mary and Joseph, the parents, and the baby Jesus.

CHI: Oh . . . Jesus, have heard of him . . . great teacher.

DOROTHY: Uh . . . yes.

DANIEL *(comes running in, pointing, excited)*: Grandma . . . Is this the one?

NANCY *(trying to keep up)*: Yes, Daniel . . . this is the one.

DANIEL: Look, Grandma . . . there He is!

NANCY: Yes, Daniel . . . the baby Jesus . . . or at least a pretend little baby doll. *(Beat)* But it doesn't matter . . . it's the fact that they actually tried to show Him that matters.

CHI *(to DANIEL, said as if he knew all along)*: Yes, and there is Mary and Joseph.

DANIEL: Isn't it great? We come here every year, and we've never seen a window like this!

CHI: Why?

DANIEL: All the other ones are shiny and full of neat stuff to buy. But this year they have the real thing!

CHI: The real thing?

DOROTHY: Oh, those sheep do look real, don't they? But I think they're just pretend.

DANIEL: No, I mean they have the real Christmas . . . Jesus and His mom and dad . . . you know, when He first came as a baby!

DOROTHY: Oh, yes, of course.

CHI: Of course . . .

NANCY: Daniel, look, the sheep are almost smiling.

DANIEL: Because they knew, Grandma.

CHI: They knew?

DANIEL: Yeah, . . . they knew that finally the real Lamb had come . . . the Lamb of God . . . *(Points up)* Look, even the star knew, it's shining.

DOROTHY: It's all coming back . . .

CHI: But where is the Santa?

DANIEL: Oh, him. He didn't come along till a long time later. *(Beat)* He loved Jesus and kids and tried to give the poor kids gifts.

CHI *(shaking head, dumbfounded):* This is not what I have been taught . . .

VIC *(enters, huffing and puffing):* Daniel, you're too fast for me.

NANCY *(grabs his arm):* Are you all right?

CHI *(staring incredulously at* VIC*):* Now, I am very confused.

DANIEL *(to* VIC*):* Sorry, I just couldn't wait to see it!

VIC *(looks at display):* It is beautiful. *(Pause)* I'm so glad somebody finally had the courage to do it!

CHI: Excuse me, but . . . are you on your lunch break?

VIC *(laughs):* Oh, no . . . *(whisks off hat)* But would you care to join us for lunch?

NANCY *(to* DOROTHY*):* And you, too, if you're free?

DOROTHY: Well . . . *(hesitantly)* I have a friend waiting for me up ahead . . .

NANCY: Then bring her, too.

DOROTHY: Thank you . . . that's very generous . . . I don't know if . . . well, *(to* DANIEL*)* Daniel, right? I have some questions . . . and . . . you seem to be full of answers. All this has me thinking about times past, times I've missed. Do you mind if I sit next to you at lunch?

VIC: A great way to spend the time, meeting new friends . . . talking about things we've seen. *(Said with a twinkle in his eye)* Glad you waited for us. (NANCY *takes* DOROTHY *by the arm and* VIC *puts arm around* CHI's *shoulder as they exit.)*

The end